Our
Mexican Fiesta
Recipes

Copyright 2012, Gooseberry Patch
First Printing, September, 2012

Add whimsy to your breakfast table with vintage
salt & pepper shakers in fun shapes. Look for 'em
at yard sales, or bring your grandmother's
old shakers out of the cupboard.

Huevos Rancheros

1 c. refried beans	1 c. shredded Cheddar cheese
2 T. oil	8 slices bacon, crisply cooked
4 6-inch corn tortillas	and crumbled
4 eggs	1/2 c. salsa

Place beans in a microwave-safe dish. Cover and microwave on high setting until heated through; set aside. Heat oil in a small skillet over medium-high heat. Add tortillas to skillet, one at a time, until firm but not crisp. Drain on paper towels. Break eggs into skillet; lower heat and cook as desired, over easy or sunny-side up. Arrange tortillas on 4 plates. Spread tortillas with beans; top with egg, cheese, bacon and salsa.

Whip up some special hot cocoa with a round disc of
Mexican chocolate...it has cinnamon and sugar already
mixed in! Bring 4 cups milk almost to a boil, add the chocolate
and whisk until it's melted and creamy.

Egg & Bacon Quesadillas

Serves 4

2 T. butter, divided
4 8-inch flour tortillas
5 eggs
1/2 c. milk
8-oz. pkg. shredded Cheddar
    cheese

6 to 8 slices bacon, crisply cooked
    and crumbled
Optional: salsa, sour cream

Lightly spread about 1/4 teaspoon butter on one side of each tortilla; set aside. In a bowl, beat eggs and milk until combined. Pour egg mixture into a hot, lightly greased skillet; cook and stir over medium heat until set. Remove scrambled eggs to a dish and keep warm. Melt remaining butter in the skillet and add a tortilla, buttered-side down. Layer with 1/4 of the cheese, 1/2 of the eggs and 1/2 of the bacon. Top with 1/4 of the cheese and a tortilla, buttered-side up. Cook one to 2 minutes on each side, until golden. Repeat with remaining ingredients. Cut each into 4 wedges and serve with salsa and sour cream, if desired.

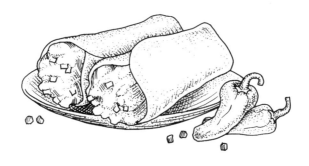

Eating breakfast on the run? Any egg dish turns into a portable breakfast when rolled up in a flour tortilla.

Breakfast Burritos

Makes 8 servings

16-oz. pkg. ground pork
   breakfast sausage
8-oz. pkg. shredded Mexican-
   blend cheese

10-oz. can diced tomatoes with
   green chiles, drained
5 eggs, beaten
8 10-inch flour tortillas

Brown sausage in a skillet over medium heat; drain. In a bowl, combine sausage, cheese and tomatoes. Cook eggs in the skillet over low heat until set. Add eggs to sausage mixture and mix thoroughly. Divide mixture evenly among tortillas and roll up tightly. Seal tortillas by cooking for one to 2 minutes on a hot griddle sprayed with non-stick vegetable spray.

Bring out the cast-iron skillet you got from
your Abuelita. (That's Spanish for Granny!) If the skillet
hasn't been used in awhile, season it first...rub it
all over with oil and bake at 300 degrees for an hour.
Cool completely and it's ready to use.

Pepper Jack Frittata

Makes 4 servings

1 red pepper, chopped
1 green pepper, chopped
1 t. fresh parsley, chopped

3/4 c. shredded Pepper Jack
   cheese
6 eggs, beaten

Sprinkle peppers, parsley and cheese into a 9" pie plate coated with butter-flavored non-stick vegetable spray. Pour eggs over all. Bake at 375 degrees for 30 minutes, until set. Cut into wedges.

☑ tortillas
☑ spicy salsa
☑ pinto beans
☑ chili peppers

Visit a local Mexican grocery, called a tienda, or stroll
the Mexican food aisle in your favorite supermarket!
You're sure to be inspired by a world of flavorful foods.

Fiesta Enchiladas

Serves 6

8-oz. pkg. shredded Cheddar
   cheese
1 onion, chopped
1/4 c. sliced black olives

1 T. oil
24 6-inch corn tortillas
2 10-oz. cans enchilada sauce
4 c. cooked turkey, chopped

Combine cheese, onion and olives in a small bowl; set aside. Heat oil in a skillet over medium heat; add tortillas, a few at a time, and cook until soft. Dip tortillas in sauce to coat. Spoon turkey and cheese mixture into center of each tortilla; roll up and place 12 enchiladas in a lightly greased 13"x9" baking pan. Spread enough of remaining sauce to cover. Make a second layer of enchiladas; spread remaining sauce on top and sprinkle with remaining cheese mixture. Bake, uncovered, at 350 degrees for 20 minutes, or until cheese is melted.

Some like it hot...try using extra-spicy salsa and
Mexican-flavor cheese spread for extra zing!

Kimberly's Taquito Bake

Serves 8 to 10

22-1/2 oz. pkg. frozen flour
    chicken & cheese taquitos
10-3/4 oz. can cream of
    mushroom soup
10-oz. can diced tomatoes with
    green chiles

10-oz. can green enchilada sauce
8-oz. pkg. shredded Colby Jack
    cheese
Garnish: sour cream, salsa,
    tortilla chips

Arrange frozen taquitos in a single layer in a 13"x9" baking pan sprayed with non-stick vegetable spray; set aside. Mix together soup, tomatoes with chiles and sauce; spoon mixture over taquitos. Bake, uncovered, at 350 degrees for 25 to 30 minutes, until cheese melts. Serve garnished with sour cream, salsa and tortilla chips on the side.

Toting a casserole to a get-together? Wrap it up
in a cheery bandanna and tie the knot at the top...
an ideal spot to slip in a serving spoon!

Renae's Taco Casserole

1 lb. ground beef
1-1/4 oz. pkg. taco seasoning mix
15-oz. can tomato sauce
3 c. elbow macaroni, cooked

8-oz. container sour cream
1 c. shredded Cheddar cheese,
    divided
1/4 c. grated Parmesan cheese

In a skillet over medium heat, brown beef. Drain; stir in taco seasoning and tomato sauce. Bring to a boil and remove from heat. In a bowl, combine cooked macaroni, sour cream and 1/2 cup Cheddar cheese. Spoon macaroni mixture into a lightly greased 13"x9" baking pan. Top with beef mixture and remaining cheeses. Bake, uncovered, at 350 degrees for 30 minutes, or until hot and bubbly.

Looking to save a few calories? It's so easy
when serving Mexican-style foods. Reduced-calorie
sour cream and low-fat cheeses are perfect
garnishes that taste great.

Chicken Chilaquiles

Makes 6 to 8 servings

1/2 c. oil
10 6-inch corn tortillas, cut into
    1/2-inch strips
Optional: salt to taste
1 c. shredded mozzarella cheese

1 c. shredded Cheddar cheese
2 c. cooked chicken, shredded
28-oz. can mild chile verde sauce,
    divided

Heat oil in a skillet over medium heat, until hot. Cook tortilla strips,
a few at a time, just until crisp. Drain tortilla strips on paper towels;
sprinkle with salt, if desired. Mix cheeses in a bowl; set aside. Spray a
13"x9" baking pan with non-stick vegetable spray. Layer half of the
tortilla strips in pan; top with chicken, one cup sauce and one cup cheese
mixture. Press layers gently down into pan. Repeat layering with
remaining tortilla strips, sauce and cheese. Bake, uncovered, at
350 degrees for about 30 minutes, until cheese is melted and golden.

Dress up the table south-of-the-border style...
arrange colorful woven blankets, sombreros
and tissue paper flowers around the room!

Shirl's Awesome Burritos

Serves 4 to 6

1 to 2 lbs. ground beef
1 onion, chopped
16-oz. can refried beans with
    green chiles
16-oz. jar chunky salsa, divided
8-oz. pkg. shredded Cheddar
    cheese, divided

salt and pepper to taste
16 to 20 8-inch flour tortillas,
    warmed
2 to 3 T. butter, melted
Garnish: sour cream, salsa

In a saucepan over medium heat, brown beef with onion. Drain; stir in beans, one cup salsa, one cup cheese, salt and pepper. Cook for a few minutes, until cheese is melted; remove from heat. With an ice cream scoop, place 2 scoops beef mixture in the center of each warmed tortilla. Roll up tortillas; place seam-side down in 2 lightly buttered 13"x9" baking pans. Brush lightly with butter; top with remaining salsa and cheese. Bake, uncovered, at 350 degrees for 10 to 15 minutes, until heated through and cheese is melted. Serve with sour cream and salsa.

Corn and flour tortillas come in several different sizes and types. Here's a handy size guide:

6-inch tortillas = tacos

8-inch tortillas = fajitas

10-inch tortillas = burritos

Cheesy Corn & Bean Burritos

Serves 6 to 8

15-oz. can black beans, drained
    and rinsed
16-oz. can corn, drained
8-oz. can chopped green chiles,
    drained
12-oz. pkg. shredded Monterey
    Jack cheese, divided

1 bunch fresh cilantro, chopped
    and divided
2 c. cooked rice
6 to 8 10-inch flour tortillas
16-oz. jar salsa, divided

Combine beans, corn, chiles, 2 cups cheese and half of the chopped cilantro; stir in cooked rice. Spoon 1/2 cup bean mixture along the center of each tortilla; top with 2 tablespoons salsa. Roll up burrito-style and arrange seam-side down in a greased 13"x9" baking pan. Spread any remaining bean mixture over burritos. Spoon remaining salsa over burritos and into corners of pan; top with remaining cheese. Cover loosely with aluminum foil. Bake at 425 degrees for 30 minutes, or until heated through and cheese has melted. Garnish with remaining cilantro, as desired.

Fix a double batch! Brown two pounds of ground beef
with two packages of taco seasoning mix, then freeze
half of the mixture for a quick meal another night.
What a time-saver!

Mexican Skillet Spaghetti

Serves 4 to 6

1 lb. ground beef chuck
15-oz. can tomato sauce
3 c. plus 2 T. water
2 1-1/4 oz. pkgs. taco seasoning
    mix

2 T. onion, minced
8-oz. pkg. spaghetti, uncooked
    and broken up
1/2 c. shredded Cheddar cheese

Brown beef in a skillet over medium heat; drain. Stir in sauce, water, taco seasoning and onion. Bring to a boil; reduce heat and simmer, covered, until spaghetti is tender, about 25 to 30 minutes. Sprinkle with cheese; let stand until cheese melts.

It's a cinch to warm tortillas for your favorite Mexican dish.
Place several tortillas on a microwave-safe plate and cover
with a dampened paper towel. Microwave on high for
30 seconds to one minute.

Fajitas with Grilled Vegetables

Makes 8 servings

1 lb. beef sirloin steak
2 green, red and/or yellow
    peppers, halved
1 zucchini, cut lengthwise
1 yellow squash, cut lengthwise
4 thick slices red onion
3/4 c. salsa
2 T. olive oil

2 T. lime juice
2 T. tequila or water
2 cloves garlic, minced
8 8-inch flour tortillas, warmed
Garnish: shredded Mexican-blend
    cheese, salsa, guacamole,
    sour cream

Place steak and vegetables in a large plastic zipping bag. Whisk together salsa, oil, lime juice, tequila or water and garlic; pour into bag. Close bag securely; turn to coat steak and vegetables. Refrigerate at least 2 hours, turning occasionally. Remove steak and vegetables from bag, reserving marinade. In a small saucepan, bring remaining marinade to a boil; remove from heat. Place steak and vegetables on a hot grill, 4 to 5 inches from heat. Grill for about 5 minutes on each side, to desired doneness. Slice steak, peppers and squash into thin strips. Separate onion into rings. Divide steak and vegetables among tortillas. Drizzle with warm marinade; add desired toppings and roll up.

Need some cooked chicken for tacos and there's none to be had? Boneless chicken breasts sauté quickly if pounded thin with a meat mallet or even a small heavy skillet. Place chicken in a large plastic zipping bag first for no-mess convenience.

Chicken Chimies

Serves 6 to 8

2 boneless, skinless chicken
    breasts, cooked and shredded
garlic salt and pepper to taste
1 to 2 T. butter
10 8-inch flour tortillas
8-oz. pkg. shredded Monterey
    Jack cheese

1/4 c. green onion, diced
1 T. oil
Garnish: refried beans,
    sour cream, guacamole

Sprinkle chicken with garlic salt and pepper. Heat butter in a large skillet over medium heat; add chicken and sauté for about 3 minutes. Spoon chicken into each tortilla. Top with cheese and green onion; roll up. Heat oil in a large skillet over medium-high heat. Add rolled-up tortillas, seam-side down; sauté until golden. Serve with refried beans, sour cream and guacamole.

Whip up a zippy Tex-Mex side dish pronto! Prepare
instant rice, using chicken broth instead of water.
Stir in a generous dollop of spicy salsa, top with
shredded cheese and cover until cheese melts.

Family-Favorite Pork Tacos

Serves 4

2 t. oil
1 lb. pork tenderloin, cubed
1 t. ground cumin
2 cloves garlic, minced
1 c. green or red salsa
Optional: 1/2 c. fresh cilantro, chopped

8 10-inch corn tortillas, warmed
Garnish: shredded lettuce, diced tomatoes, sliced avocado, sliced black olives, sour cream, shredded Cheddar cheese

Heat oil in a non-stick skillet over medium-high heat. Add pork cubes and cumin; cook until golden on all sides, about 5 minutes. Add garlic and cook for one minute; drain. Stir in salsa and heat through; stir in cilantro, if using. Using 2 forks, shred pork. Fill warmed tortillas with pork mixture; garnish as desired.

Salsa in a jiffy! Pour a can of stewed tomatoes,
several slices of canned jalapeño peppers and
a teaspoon or two of the jalapeño juice into a blender.
Cover and process to the desired consistency.

Light & Healthy Fish Tacos

Serves 4

4 fillets mahi-mahi, halibut or
    other mild white fish
4 to 8 6-inch flour tortillas

Garnish: shredded Cheddar-Jack
    cheese, shredded cabbage,
    salsa, lime wedges

Grill fish as desired. When fish flakes easily, slice each fillet into 2 long pieces. Warm tortillas in a skillet. To serve, fill each tortilla with a piece of fish, some cheese and some cabbage, a dollop of salsa and a squeeze of lime juice.

Fresh hot peppers from your own garden or
a nearby farmers' market are extra flavorful,
but take care when slicing them. It's best to wear
rubber gloves, and be sure not to touch your eyes.

Cream Cheese Enchiladas

Makes 8 servings

2 8-oz. pkgs. cream cheese,
  softened
8-oz. container sour cream
2 10-oz. cans mild green
  enchilada sauce
1/4 c. jalapeño peppers, seeded
  and chopped
1 lb. ground beef, browned and
  drained

1/2 c. shredded sharp Cheddar
  cheese
1 sweet onion, chopped
1/2 c. sliced black olives
8 8-inch flour tortillas
Garnish: sliced black olives,
  chopped tomato, shredded
  lettuce, chopped green onion

In a large bowl, blend together cream cheese, sour cream, sauce and jalapeños; set aside. Combine beef and shredded cheese in another bowl; set aside. Fill each tortilla with one to 2 tablespoons cream cheese mixture and one to 2 tablespoons beef mixture. Sprinkle each with onion and olives; roll up tortillas. Place seam-side down in a greased 13"x9" baking pan; cover with remaining cream cheese mixture. Bake, uncovered, at 400 degrees for 30 to 40 minutes; cover if top begins to brown. Garnish as desired.

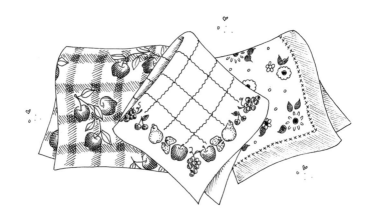

Saucy tacos and burritos are best served on a
vintage-style oilcloth...spills wipe right up! Look for one
with a colorful design of fruit or flowers.

Anytime Enchurritos

Makes 6 to 8 servings

2 c. turkey, cooked and shredded
1-1/2 c. salsa, divided
8-oz. container sour cream
2 to 3 T. diced green chiles
8 10-inch flour tortillas

10-3/4 oz. can cream of chicken
soup
8-oz. pkg. shredded Mexican-
blend cheese

Combine turkey, 1/2 cup salsa, sour cream and chiles. Spoon turkey mixture into tortillas; roll up and place seam-side down in a greased 13"x9" baking pan. Blend together soup and remaining salsa; spoon over tortillas. Bake, uncovered, at 350 degrees for 30 minutes. Sprinkle with cheese and bake an additional 5 minutes, or until cheese is melted.

Serve up icy lemonade in frosted-rim glasses! Chill tumblers in the fridge. At serving time, moisten rims with lemon juice or water and dip into a dish of sparkling sugar.

JoAnn's Travelin' Tacos

Makes 8 servings

1 lb. ground beef
1-1/4 oz. pkg. taco seasoning mix
8 1-oz. pkgs. corn chips
2 c. lettuce, chopped
1 tomato, chopped

1/2 c. sliced black olives
1 c. shredded Cheddar cheese
1/2 c. sour cream
1/2 c. salsa

Brown beef in a skillet over medium heat; drain. Stir in taco seasoning and prepare according to package directions. Gently crush corn chips inside unopened bags, then cut each bag open along one side edge. Spoon equal amounts of ground beef and remaining ingredients into each bag. Serve right in the bag with a fork.

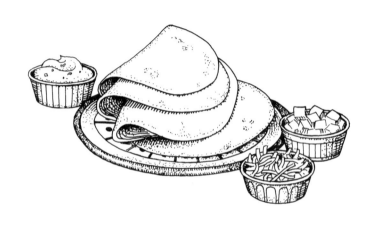

He who divides and shares is left with the best share.

— Mexican Proverb

Slow-Cooker Chicken Tacolados

Serves 6 to 8

5 boneless, skinless chicken
    thighs
2 boneless, skinless chicken
    breasts
10-oz. can green enchilada sauce
10-3/4 oz. can cream of chicken
    soup

12 to 15 10-inch flour tortillas,
    warmed
Garnish: salsa, shredded Cheddar
    cheese

Arrange chicken pieces in a slow cooker; set aside. Combine sauce and soup in a bowl; blend well and pour over chicken. Cover and cook on low setting for 8 hours, or on high setting for 4 hours. When chicken is tender, shred with 2 forks. Serve on warmed tortillas; garnish as desired.

All-day slow cooking is ideal for less-tender cuts of
meat like pork shoulder and beef chuck roast.
They'll turn out juicy and falling-apart tender...
just right for many Mexican dishes.

Savory Pork Carnitas

Makes 8 servings

3 to 4-lb. Boston butt pork roast
1-1/4 oz. pkg. taco seasoning mix
3 cloves garlic, sliced
1 onion, quartered
4-oz. can diced green chiles
3/4 to 1 c. water

6 to 8 flour tortillas
Garnish: shredded lettuce,
chopped tomatoes, sliced
avocado, sour cream, lime
wedges, sliced green onions,
fresh cilantro sprigs

Combine pork, taco seasoning, garlic, onion and chiles in a slow cooker.
Add water, using the full amount if pork is closer to 4 pounds; stir to
combine. Cover and cook for 10 hours on low setting, or 6 hours on high
setting, until tender enough to shred. Spoon shredded pork down center
of tortillas. Fold and serve with desired garnishes.

Paper coffee filters make tidy holders for tacos
and tortilla wraps...easy for little hands to hold too.

Carne Guisada

2-lb. beef rump roast, trimmed
    and cubed
salt and pepper to taste
2 lbs. potatoes, peeled and
    chopped
10-3/4 oz. can cream of
    mushroom and roasted
    garlic soup

4-oz. can chopped green chiles
1 t. ground cumin
flour tortillas
Garnish: guacamole, shredded
    Cheddar cheese

Sprinkle beef cubes with salt and pepper. Combine with remaining
ingredients in a slow cooker. Cover and cook on low for 8 to 10 hours.
If desired, mash lightly with a potato masher after cooking. Serve beef
mixture on warmed tortillas, topped with guacamole and cheese. May
also be served as a main dish with warm cornbread and simmered greens.

Prop a mini chalkboard next to the slow cooker...it's just right for announcing what's for dinner and what time it will be ready.

Sweet Pork Barbacoa

Serves 10 to 12

3-lb. boneless pork tenderloin
3 c. mild, medium or hot salsa
3/4 c. cola

1 c. brown sugar, packed
salt and pepper to taste

Place tenderloin in a slow cooker. Mix remaining ingredients and pour over tenderloin. Cover and cook on low setting for 8 hours, or until very tender. Remove pork and shred with 2 forks. Return pork to slow cooker; stir to mix with juices. Serve pork as desired in burritos, toasted rolls or taco salads.

If you love super-spicy chili, give New Mexico chili powder a try.
It contains pure ground red chili peppers, unlike regular chili
powder which is a blend of chili, garlic and other seasonings.

Mexican Albondigas Soup

Serves 8

2 lbs. lean ground beef
1 c. Italian-seasoned dry bread
  crumbs
1 egg, beaten
3 stalks celery, sliced
1 green pepper, diced
1 c. carrot, peeled and diced
15-1/4 oz. can corn, drained
2 14-oz. cans beef broth
10-oz. can diced tomatoes with
  green chiles

4-oz. can diced green chiles
3 c. cooked rice
2 T. fresh cilantro, finely chopped
2 T. onion, minced
1 t. garlic powder
1 t. ground cumin
1 t. chili powder
1 t. salt
1/2 t. pepper
4 to 5 c. water

Combine beef, bread crumbs and egg; form into one-inch balls. Brown in a skillet over medium heat; drain. Place meatballs in a slow cooker and set aside. In a small saucepan, cover celery, green pepper and carrot with a little water. Cook until tender; add to slow cooker with remaining ingredients. Cover and cook on low setting for 3 to 4 hours, stirring occasionally.

Treat yourself to crisp savory crackers with soup.
Spread saltines with softened butter, then sprinkle lightly with
chili powder, paprika or another favorite spice. Pop into a
350-degree oven just until golden, 3 to 6 minutes.

Slow-Cooker White Chili

Serves 6 to 8

16-oz. pkg. dried Great Northern
    beans
2 lbs. boneless, skinless chicken
    breasts, cubed
14-1/2 oz. can chicken broth
1 c. water
1 onion, chopped

3 cloves garlic, minced
2 4-oz. cans chopped green chiles
2 t. ground cumin
1-1/2 t. cayenne pepper
1 t. dried oregano
1/2 t. salt

Soak beans in water overnight; drain. Combine all ingredients in a slow cooker and stir. Cover and cook on low setting for 10 to 12 hours, or on high setting for 5 to 6 hours, stirring occasionally.

There's no such thing as too much chili! Spoon chili into flour tortillas and sprinkle with shredded cheese for quick burritos or quesadillas.

Kathleen's Fabulous Chili

Serves 6 to 8

1 lb. ground beef
1/2 to 1 lb. bacon, chopped
1 onion, chopped
1/2 green pepper, diced
2 15-oz. cans dark red kidney
   beans, drained and rinsed
16-oz. can light red kidney beans,
   drained and rinsed
16-oz. can pinto beans, drained
   and rinsed
16-oz. can pork & beans
15-1/2 oz. can Sloppy Joe sauce
14-1/2 oz. can diced tomatoes,
   drained and juice reserved
1/4 to 1/2 c. brown sugar, packed
salt, pepper and chili powder
   to taste

Brown beef and bacon with onion and green pepper; drain. Combine all ingredients in a slow cooker, using half of reserved tomato juice; cover and cook on high setting until chili just begins to simmer, about one hour. Reduce to low setting; continue to cook for 2 to 4 hours. If more liquid is needed, use remaining tomato juice.

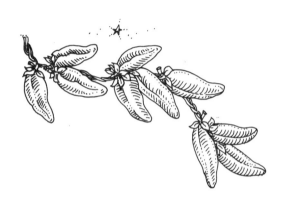

Hot, hot, hot! If a dish proves just too hot for your taste,
reach for a glass of milk, not water...it's much better
for cooling the heat. Nibbling on a flour tortilla or
a slice of bread may help quench the flames too.

Chile Verde Soup

Serves 6 to 8

1/2 lb. pork tenderloin, cut into
    1/2-inch cubes
1 t. oil
2 c. chicken broth
2 15-oz. cans white beans,
    drained and rinsed

2 4-oz. cans diced green chiles
1/4 t. ground cumin
1/4 t. dried oregano
salt and pepper to taste
6 to 8 sprigs fresh cilantro

In a skillet over medium heat, brown pork in oil for one to 2 minutes;
drain. Place pork in a slow cooker. Add remaining ingredients; stir. Cover
and cook on low setting for 4 to 6 hours.

Stem and seed a sweet pepper in a flash...hold the pepper
upright on a cutting board. Use a sharp knife to slice
each of the sides from the pepper. You'll then have
four large seedless pieces ready for chopping!

Mexican Vegetable Chili

Makes 6 to 8 servings

1 c. jicama, peeled and diced
1 c. onion, chopped
1/2 c. celery, chopped
1/2 c. carrot, peeled and sliced
1 green pepper, chopped
2 cloves garlic, minced
2 t. oil
1/2 c. water
2 t. beef bouillon granules
1-1/2 t. ground cumin

1-1/2 t. chili powder
8-oz. can no-salt-added tomato
    sauce
2 14-1/2 oz. cans no-salt-added
    whole tomatoes
15-oz. can chili beans
15-oz. can pinto beans, drained
    and rinsed
Garnish: shredded Cheddar
    cheese

In a Dutch oven over medium heat, sauté jicama, onion, celery, carrots, green pepper and garlic in oil until crisp-tender. Stir in water, bouillon granules, seasonings and tomato sauce. Add whole tomatoes with their juice, cutting or breaking up tomatoes. Reduce heat to low; cover and simmer for 20 minutes, stirring occasionally. Uncover; simmer an additional 10 to 20 minutes, or until vegetables are tender. Stir in beans; simmer until heated through. Serve topped with cheese.

Crunchy tortilla strips are a tasty addition to southwestern-style soups. Cut corn tortillas into thin strips, then deep-fry quickly. Drain on paper towels before sprinkling over bowls of soup. Try red or blue tortilla chips too!

One-Pot Spicy Black Bean Chili

Makes 4 servings

1 onion, chopped
2 t. garlic, minced
2 t. olive oil
3 16-oz. cans black beans,
    drained and rinsed
16-oz. pkg. frozen corn
14-1/2 oz. can diced tomatoes
    with green chiles
1/2 c. water

1-1/2 t. taco seasoning mix
7-oz. can chipotle chiles in
    adobo sauce
1 T. rice vinegar
1/4 c. fresh cilantro, chopped
1/4 c. reduced-fat sour cream
Optional: salsa, fresh cilantro
    sprigs

In a saucepan, sauté onion and garlic in oil for 5 to 7 minutes, until onion softens and begins to brown. Add beans, corn, tomatoes, water and taco seasoning. Bring to a boil; reduce heat to low and simmer for about 15 minutes, stirring occasionally. Combine chiles in sauce and vinegar in a blender; process until puréed. Stir chile mixture and cilantro into chili, adding more taco seasoning if a spicier chili is preferred; heat through. Divide into soup bowls; top with dollops of sour cream. Garnish with salsa and a sprig of cilantro, if desired.

Bake some crisp cornbread sticks...fun to dip in chili!
Simply stir up a corn muffin mix, pour into a cast-iron cornstick
pan and bake according to package directions.

Chicken Enchilada Soup

Serves 6 to 8

3 14-oz. cans chicken broth
3 10-3/4 oz. cans cream of
    chicken soup
4-oz. can chopped mild green
    chiles

2 c. cooked chicken, diced
1/2 t. chili powder
16-oz. pkg. pasteurized process
    cheese spread, cubed
Garnish: tortilla chips

In a stockpot, mix all ingredients except cheese and garnish. Cook over medium heat until smooth, about 10 to 15 minutes, stirring occasionally. Reduce heat to low; add cheese. Simmer without boiling until cheese has melted; keep stirring to prevent sticking to bottom of pan. To serve, line soup bowls with tortilla chips; ladle soup over chips.

Canned yellow or white hominy makes a tasty, filling addition to any southwestern-style soup.

Easy Taco Soup

1 lb. ground beef
14-1/2 oz. can beef broth
16-oz. can pinto beans
16-oz. can black beans
15-1/4 oz. can corn
10-oz. can diced tomatoes with
    green chiles
1 yellow squash, chopped
1 zucchini, chopped
2 c. water
1-1/4 oz. pkg. taco seasoning mix
1-oz. pkg. ranch salad dressing
    mix
2 T. fresh cilantro, chopped
salt and pepper to taste

In a large stockpot over medium heat, cook beef until browned; drain.
Stir in remaining ingredients. Reduce heat and simmer until squash and
zucchini are tender, about 15 minutes.

Cheesy quesadillas are quick and filling paired with a
bowl of soup. Sprinkle a flour tortilla with shredded cheese,
top with another tortilla and toast lightly in a skillet until
the cheese melts. Cut into wedges and serve with salsa.

Sweet Corn Cake

1/2 c. butter, softened
1/3 c. masa harina flour
1/4 c. water
10-oz. pkg. frozen corn, thawed
1/3 c. sugar

3 T. yellow cornmeal
2 T. whipping cream
1/4 t. baking powder
1/4 t. salt

With an electric mixer on medium speed, beat butter in a large bowl until creamy. Gradually add flour; beat in water and set aside. Place corn in a food processor or blender. Pulse to chop coarsely; stir into butter mixture. Mix remaining ingredients well; stir into butter mixture. Pour into a greased 8"x8" baking pan; cover with aluminum foil. Set in a 13"x9" baking pan; add water 1/3 of the way up around small pan. Bake at 350 degrees for 50 to 60 minutes. Uncover; let stand for 15 minutes. Scoop with a small scoop; serve warm.

Treat everyone to honey-pecan butter with warm sopapillas or corn muffins. Simply blend together 1/2 cup butter, 1/2 cup honey and 1/3 cup toasted chopped pecans. Delectable!

Golden Sopapillas

Makes one dozen

1-3/4 c. all-purpose flour
2 t. baking powder
1 t. salt

2 T. shortening
2/3 c. cold water
oil for deep frying

In a bowl, mix flour, baking powder and salt. Cut in shortening with a pastry cutter until mixture resembles cornmeal. Add water, one tablespoon at a time, until a stiff dough forms; set aside. Add 4 inches of oil to a deep fryer; heat to about 375 degrees. While oil heats, roll out dough on a floured surface until very thin. Cut into 4-inch squares. Test oil by dropping in a small piece of dough; if dough browns quickly, it's ready. Fry each piece until it puffs up; turn over carefully and fry until other side is golden. Lift out with a slotted spoon; drain on paper towels. Serve warm.

A generous square of checked homespun or flowered calico
makes a cozy liner for a basket of warm muffins or sopapillas.

Corn & Green Chile Muffins

Makes one dozen

1-1/4 c. cornmeal
1/2 t. salt
2 t. baking powder
1 c. shredded sharp Cheddar
    cheese
8-oz. can creamed corn

4-oz. can chopped green chiles,
    drained
8-oz. container sour cream
2 eggs, beaten
1/4 c. canola oil

Combine cornmeal, salt and baking powder in a bowl; mix well. Stir in cheese, corn, chiles and sour cream. Add eggs and oil; stir just until combined. Spoon batter into a muffin tin that has been sprayed with non-stick vegetable spray, filling each cup about 1/2 full. Bake at 400 degrees for about 20 minutes, until golden.

Serve fresh salads in crisp tortilla bowls. Spray non-stick vegetable spray on one side of a corn tortilla and on the inside of an oven-safe bowl. Gently press the tortilla into the bowl, sprayed-side up. Bake at 350 degrees for 15 minutes, or until golden. Cool before filling.

Guacamole Tossed Salad

Makes 4 servings

2 tomatoes, chopped
1/2 red onion, sliced and
    separated into rings
6 slices bacon, crisply cooked
    and crumbled
1/3 c. oil
2 T. cider vinegar

1 t. salt
1/4 t. pepper
1/4 t. hot pepper sauce
2 avocados, halved, pitted
    and cubed
4 c. salad greens, torn

In a bowl, combine tomatoes, onion and bacon. In a separate bowl, whisk together oil, vinegar, salt, pepper and hot pepper sauce. Pour over tomato mixture; toss gently. Add avocados. Place greens in a large serving bowl; add avocado mixture and toss to coat. Serve immediately.

Hollowed-out bell peppers make fun salad bowls! Whether it's a crisp green salad or a mixed vegetable salad, they're just the right size and add a splash of color to the table.

Aztec Salad

2 16-oz. cans black beans,
   drained and rinsed
1 sweet onion, diced
2 tomatoes, diced

15-1/4 oz. can corn, drained
1 green pepper, diced
1 red pepper, diced

Combine all ingredients in a large bowl; toss with Spicy Dressing. Cover and chill; stir again before serving.

Spicy Dressing:

2 T. rice vinegar
2 T. cider vinegar
3 T. lemon juice
2 cloves garlic, minced

2 t. dried cumin
1 t. dried cilantro
1/8 t. cayenne pepper

Whisk together all ingredients in a small bowl.

Spice up your favorite ranch salad dressing. To one cup of
ranch salad dressing, add 1/4 teaspoon chili powder and
1/2 teaspoon ground cumin. Let stand for 5 minutes so
flavors can blend. Terrific on salads...for dipping too!

Mexican Confetti Salad

Serves 6

3 c. frozen corn, cooked and
  drained
3 tomatoes, chopped
2 green peppers, chopped

15-oz. can black beans, drained
  and rinsed
1/3 c. fresh cilantro, chopped

Combine all ingredients in a serving bowl. Drizzle with Lime Dressing; toss gently. Chill until serving time.

Lime Dressing:

3 T. lime juice
1 t. garlic, minced
1 t. salt

1 t. pepper
1/4 c. olive oil

Whisk together all ingredients in a small bowl.

For hearty salads in a snap, keep cans of diced tomatoes, black olives, beans and sweet corn in the fridge. They'll be chilled and ready to toss with fresh greens and salad dressing at a moment's notice.

Corn-Avocado Salad

Serves 4

16-oz. pkg. frozen corn, thawed
1 tomato, diced
2 T. fresh cilantro, chopped
2 T. lime juice
1 T. olive oil

1/4 t. salt
1/4 t. sugar
1 avocado, halved, pitted
   and diced

In a bowl, combine all ingredients except avocado; mix well. Fold in avocado; cover and chill before serving.

Pumpkin seeds are crunchy and tasty sprinkled over salads.
Look for them year 'round in the Mexican food section,
where they're labeled as "pepitas."

Ranchero Chicken & Bean Salad

Serves 2 to 4

3/4 c. ranch salad dressing
2 T. fresh cilantro, chopped
1/2 t. chili powder
1 t. lime juice
15-oz. can black beans, drained
    and rinsed
11-oz. can sweet corn & diced
    peppers, drained

1 red pepper, sliced into
    thin strips
1/3 c. green onion, sliced
6 c. romaine lettuce, torn
1-1/2 c. cooked chicken, sliced
    into strips

Combine salad dressing, cilantro, chili powder and lime juice in a small bowl; stir well and set aside. In a large salad bowl, toss together beans, corn, pepper and onion. Arrange lettuce on individual serving plates; top with bean mixture and chicken strips. Drizzle with dressing and serve.

Speed prep time as well as clean up time! Chop ingredients in advance and place them in containers. Cover and store in the refrigerator until needed later.

Mexicali Bean Salad

Serves 10 to 12

16-oz. can pinto beans, drained
    and rinsed
16-oz. kidney beans, drained
    and rinsed
16-oz. can black beans, drained
    and rinsed
16-oz. can Great Northern beans,
    drained and rinsed
15-oz. can corn, drained

6-oz. can black olives, drained
    and sliced
2 tomatoes, chopped
1 c. red onion, chopped
1 bunch fresh cilantro, chopped
16-oz. bottle Italian salad
    dressing
2 limes

Combine beans and corn in a large bowl. Add olives, tomatoes, onion, cilantro and salad dressing; mix well. Squeeze the juice of one lime over salad, mixing well. Slice remaining lime and arrange around edge of salad.

First aid for casserole dishes with baked-on food spatters!
Mix equal amounts of cream of tartar and white vinegar into
a paste. Spread onto the dish and let stand for 30 minutes
to an hour. Spatters will wash off easily.

Cheesy Corn & Hominy Posole

Serves 6 to 8

1 onion, chopped
2 4-oz. cans chopped green chiles
10-3/4 oz. can cream of
     mushroom soup
3 c. shredded Cheddar cheese

2 15-1/2 oz. cans hominy,
     drained
2 15-oz. cans shoepeg corn,
     drained

Combine onion, chiles, soup and cheese in a large bowl. Add hominy and corn; mix well. Transfer to a 13"x9" baking pan sprayed with non-stick vegetable spray. Cover with aluminum foil. Place a pan of water on the rack below pan in oven. Bake at 350 degrees for 30 minutes, or until heated through and cheese is melted.

Keep a couple of favorite side dishes on hand in the freezer
to make spur-of-the-moment entertaining easy. Pair them
with a deli roast chicken or some grilled meat for
a quick and hearty meal.

Oven-Baked Mexican Rice

Makes 4 to 6 servings

2 T. butter or olive oil
1 onion, chopped
1-1/2 c. long-cooking rice,
    uncooked

1 t. garlic, minced
2 c. chicken broth
1-1/4 c. tomato juice

Heat butter or oil in a skillet over medium heat. Add onion; cook until translucent. Add rice and garlic. Cook and stir until rice is lightly golden. Stir in remaining ingredients; bring to a boil. Transfer mixture to a greased 2-quart casserole dish. Cover and bake at 350 degrees for 25 minutes, or until rice is tender.

For the quickest-ever candlelit atmosphere, set several
lighted tea lights on the table and top them with metal
cheese graters. They'll cast the same twinkling
glow as pierced tin lanterns.

Corn Mazatlán

16-oz. can corn, drained and
    1/4 cup liquid reserved
8-oz. pkg. cream cheese, softened
16-oz. can shoepeg corn, drained

1/4 c. green pepper, chopped
1/4 c. green onions, chopped
2 4-oz. cans chopped green chiles
1 t. ground cumin

In a saucepan over low heat, combine reserved corn liquid and cream cheese. Cook and stir until smooth. Stir in remaining ingredients and heat through.

Cheese tends to turn crumbly when frozen, perfectly fine
to use in baked casserole dishes. Go ahead and stock up
when cheese is on sale... just thaw overnight in
the refrigerator before using.

Chile Relleno Squares

Makes 10 to 12 servings

7-oz. can whole or diced green
    chiles, drained
12-oz. pkg. shredded Colby
    cheese
12-oz. pkg. shredded Monterey
    Jack cheese

4 eggs, beaten
12-oz. can evaporated milk
2 T. all-purpose flour
16-oz. jar red or green salsa

Spread chiles in the bottom of a greased 13"x9" baking pan. Mix together
cheeses and spread over chiles. In a separate bowl, whisk together eggs,
evaporated milk and flour; pour over cheeses. Bake at 375 degrees for
30 minutes, or until top is golden. Spread salsa over top and bake an
additional 5 to 10 minutes.

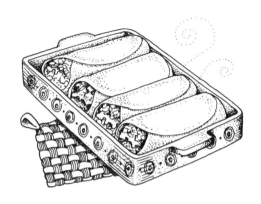

Slow-cook a pot of creamy beans. Rinse and drain 1/2 pound dried pinto beans. Place them in a slow cooker and stir in a chopped onion, a tablespoon of bacon drippings or butter and 5 cups boiling water. Cover and cook on high setting for 4 hours, stirring occasionally. Don't add salt until the beans are tender. So easy!

Unfried Refried Beans

Serves 8

16-oz. pkg. dried pinto beans
4-oz. can chopped green chiles

1 t. salt
1/2 t. chili powder

Soak beans in water overnight. Drain beans and place in a slow cooker. Add water to cover 2 inches over beans. Stir in chiles. Cover and cook on high setting for 8 hours. Drain off all but about 1/4 cup water. Stir in seasonings. Use an immersion blender to blend until smooth.

Make a trivet to protect the tabletop from hot dishes
in a jiffy. Simply attach a cork or felt square to the bottom
of a large, colorful ceramic tile with craft glue.

Corn Custard Mexicana

2 c. frozen corn, thawed
2 eggs, beaten
1 c. sour cream
1/2 c. yellow cornmeal
1 t. salt
1 T. chopped pimento

2 T. celery, chopped
4-oz. can diced green chiles
1 c. shredded Monterey Jack
   cheese
Optional: 1/2 c. butter, melted

Mix all ingredients in a large bowl. Pour into a buttered 1-1/2 quart casserole dish. Bake, covered, at 350 degrees for 45 to 50 minutes, until golden and set.

Spoon leftover Speedy Spanish Rice into
flour tortillas for a yummy quick lunch.

Speedy Spanish Rice

Serves 6

1 c. long-cooking rice, uncooked
1/2 c. onion, chopped
2 T. oil
2 c. chicken broth
3/4 c. tomato juice

1/2 t. garlic powder
1/2 t. chili powder
1/2 t. ground cumin
1/3 c. fresh cilantro, chopped

In a skillet over medium heat, sauté rice and onion in oil until onion is crisp-tender, about 5 minutes. Add remaining ingredients except cilantro. Bring to a boil; reduce heat and cover. Simmer for 15 to 20 minutes, or until liquid is absorbed. Fluff rice with a fork; fold in cilantro.

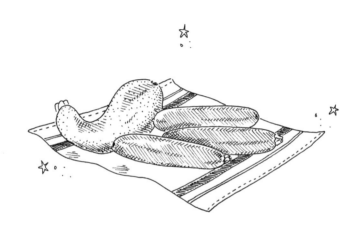

Try serving a meatless main once a week...it's economical
and healthy too. There are lots of tasty bean and
rice-based dishes to choose from.

Mexican Black-Eyed Peas

Makes 8 servings

16-oz. pkg. dried black-eyed peas
1 lb. ground pork sausage
1 onion, finely chopped
18-oz. can whole tomatoes
1/2 c. water

2-1/2 T. celery, finely chopped
2 T. sugar
2-1/2 T. chili powder
1/4 t. pepper
2 T. garlic salt

Place dried peas in a Dutch oven; add water to cover by 2 inches. Soak for 6 to 8 hours, or overnight. Brown sausage in a skillet over medium heat; drain. Add onion and cook until tender. Drain peas; stir into sausage mixture. Add tomatoes with juice and remaining ingredients except garlic salt. Bring to a boil. Cover; reduce heat and simmer for 1-1/2 hours, stirring occasionally and adding more water as necessary. Add garlic salt.

A muffin tin is useful when you're serving tacos, enchiladas
or soup with lots of tasty toppings. Fill up the sections with
shredded cheese, guacamole, diced tomatoes and sour cream...
let everyone mix & match their favorites!

Vickie's Favorite Guacamole

Makes 2 cups

4 avocados, halved and pitted
1 onion, chopped
2 cloves garlic, minced

2 T. lime juice
1/8 t. kosher salt
tortilla chips

Scoop pulp out of avocados into a bowl. Mash to desired consistency with a potato masher. Add remaining ingredients; mix well. Serve with your favorite tortilla chips.

This five-minute cheese dip can't be beat. Cut a pound of pasteurized process cheese spread into cubes and place in a microwave-safe dish. Pour a can of diced tomatoes with green chiles over top. Microwave on high setting for five minutes, stirring halfway through. Serve with crunchy tortilla chips...yum!

Salsa Roja

Makes about 3 cups

1 lb. plum tomatoes
2 T. olive oil
5 cloves garlic, chopped
1/2 c. onion, sliced and cut into
    very thin strips
1/4 c. serrano chiles, chopped
1 bunch fresh cilantro, chopped
2 T. lime juice
salt to taste
tortilla chips

Arrange tomatoes on a broiler pan or a grill; roast tomatoes until skin is blackened and tomatoes are soft. Set aside to cool. Heat oil in a skillet over medium heat. Add garlic, onion and chiles; cook until golden. Place all ingredients except salt and chips in a blender and pulse to desired thickness. Stir in salt. Serve chilled with tortilla chips.

Eating well gives a spectacular joy to life.

—Elsa Schiaparelli

Queso Blanco

Makes about 2 cups

1 c. finely shredded Monterey
    Jack cheese
4-oz. can diced green chiles
1/4 c. half-and-half
2 T. onion, finely chopped
2 t. ground cumin

1/2 t. salt
1/8 t. pepper
1 T. fresh cilantro, finely chopped
Optional: 1 serrano pepper, finely
    chopped
tortilla chips or flour tortillas

Combine all ingredients except tortillas in a double boiler. Cook over medium heat until cheese is melted and well blended, stirring occasionally. Serve warm with tortilla chips or hot flour tortillas.

Try serving lighter dippers with hearty full-flavored dips and spreads. Baked tortilla chips and fresh veggies are sturdy enough to scoop up dips yet won't overshadow the flavor of the dip.

Zesty Corn Salsa

Makes 2-1/2 cups

2 c. frozen corn, thawed
1/4 c. red pepper, chopped
2 green onions, sliced
1 jalapeño pepper, seeded
    and chopped

1 T. fresh cilantro, chopped
2 T. lime juice
1 T. oil
1/4 to 1/2 t. salt
corn chips

Combine all ingredients except corn chips; mix well. Cover; refrigerate for one hour, or until well chilled. Serve with corn chips.

Mix up your own chili powder blend! Fill a shaker with 2 teaspoons garlic powder, 2 teaspoons cumin and one teaspoon each of cayenne pepper, paprika and oregano. It's oh-so easy to adjust to your family's preference.

Best-Ever Taco Cups

Makes 10 servings

1 lb. ground beef
1-1/4 oz. pkg. taco seasoning mix
12-oz. tube refrigerated
    buttermilk biscuits

1/2 c. shredded Cheddar cheese

Brown beef in a skillet over medium heat; drain. Add taco seasoning and prepare as directed on package. Set aside. Press biscuit dough into bottoms and up sides of ungreased muffin cups; fill with seasoned beef. Bake at 400 degrees for 15 minutes. Sprinkle with cheese; return to oven and bake an additional 2 to 3 minutes, until cheese is melted.

Whip up a batch of napkins from cotton fabric in a cheery
south-of-the-border print. Cut fabric into 12-inch squares
or even 18-inch squares for lap-size napkins, then finish
with a simple hem or fringed edges...oh-so easy!

Jalapeño Poppers

Makes 2 dozen

24 pickled jalapeño peppers
1 lb. Cheddar cheese
1/2 c. cornmeal
1/2 c. all-purpose flour

1 t. salt
2 eggs, beaten
oil for deep frying

Make a short slit into each jalapeño pepper; remove as many seeds as possible. Slice cheese into strips 1/4" wide and one-inch long; insert one in each jalapeño. Combine cornmeal, flour and salt in a small bowl; place beaten eggs in a separate bowl. Dip peppers into egg mixture; roll in cornmeal mixture until well coated. Set aside on a wire rack for 30 minutes. Add 4 inches of oil to a deep fryer; heat to about 375 degrees. Add poppers in small batches; cook until crisp and golden, about 4 minutes. Remove poppers using a slotted spoon; drain on paper towels.

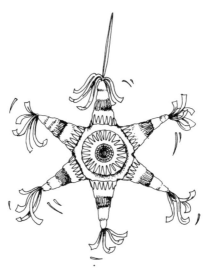

A festive piñata adds instant fun to your fiesta!
Look for new ones in all shapes and sizes...fill with
little surprises like hard candy, small toys and confetti.

4-Layer Mexican Dip

Makes 4 to 6 servings

8-oz. pkg. cream cheese, softened
15-oz. can chili with beans
16-oz. jar salsa

8-oz. pkg. shredded Mexican-
    blend cheese
tortilla chips or crackers

Spread cream cheese into the bottom of an ungreased, microwave-safe
11"x7" glass casserole dish. Layer chili, salsa and cheese on top.
Microwave on high for 5 to 7 minutes, until hot, bubbly and cheeses
are melted. Serve warm with tortilla chips or crackers for dipping.

Appetizer spreads are perfect for enjoying during
card games or a favorite movie at home with friends!
Set out a variety of creamy dips and crunchy snacks along
with fizzy beverages...then relax and enjoy your guests.

Tex-Mex Appetizer Tart

Serves 6 to 8

8-1/2 oz. pkg. corn muffin mix
3/4 c. refried beans
1/2 c. salsa
1 c. shredded Cheddar cheese

Garnish: chopped lettuce, chopped tomatoes, sliced green onion, sliced black olives, sour cream

Prepare corn muffin mix according to package directions; spread in a greased 9" round tart pan. Bake at 350 degrees for 15 minutes; set aside. Mix beans with salsa; spread over warm corn muffin crust. Sprinkle with cheese; return to oven. Bake at 350 degrees for 5 to 10 minutes, until cheese melts and beans are heated through. Layer with lettuce, tomatoes, onion and olives; top with sour cream. Cut into wedges to serve.

Curl a string of dried chile peppers into a circle,
then set a hurricane with a fat red candle in the center
for a quick and casual centerpiece.

Sangria Punch

3/4 c. sweetened lemonade
    drink mix
4 c. cranberry juice cocktail
1 c. orange juice

1 T. lime juice
3 c. club soda, chilled
2 oranges, sliced
2 limes, sliced

Empty drink mix into a large pitcher. Add juices, stirring until drink mix is completely dissolved. Refrigerate until ready to serve. At serving time, stir in club soda and sliced fruit.

"Fried" ice cream is a festive ending to a Mexican meal.
Roll scoops of ice cream in a mixture of crushed frosted corn
flake cereal and cinnamon. Garnish with a drizzle of honey and
a dollop of whipped topping. They'll ask for seconds!

Evening's End Mexicali Coffee

3/4 c. ground coffee
2 t. cinnamon
6 c. water
1 c. milk
1/3 c. chocolate syrup

2 T. light brown sugar, packed
1 t. vanilla extract
Garnish: whipped cream,
    cinnamon

Place coffee and cinnamon in the filter basket of a coffee maker. Add water and brew as usual. In a saucepan, blend milk, chocolate syrup and sugar. Stir over low heat until sugar dissolves. Combine milk mixture and brewed coffee. Stir in vanilla; garnish as desired.

Slip votives into Mason jars, then thread wire around the
jar rims to create a loop for hanging. Oh-so pretty
on a summer's evening!

Fruit Salsa & Cinnamon Chips *Makes 10 to 15 servings*

2 kiwis, peeled and diced
2 Golden Delicious apples, peeled,
    cored and diced
1/2 lb. raspberries
16-oz. pkg. strawberries, hulled
    and diced

2 c. plus 2 T. sugar, divided
1 T. brown sugar, packed
3 T. strawberry preserves
10 10-inch flour tortillas, sliced
    into wedges
1 to 2 T. cinnamon

Combine all fruit in a large bowl; mix in 2 tablespoons sugar, brown sugar and strawberry preserves. Cover and chill for at least 15 minutes. Mix together remaining sugar and cinnamon. Arrange tortilla wedges on a baking sheet; coat with butter-flavored cooking spray. Sprinkle wedges with desired amount of cinnamon-sugar. Bake at 350 degrees for 8 to 10 minutes. Repeat with remaining tortilla wedges; cool for 15 minutes. Serve chips with chilled fruit salsa.

Glass bottles of colorful Mexican soda pop are
party-perfect! Choose an assortment of zingy flavors
like watermelon, mango and pineapple just for fun.

Mexican Wedding Cookies   *Makes about 3-1/2 dozen*

1 c. butter, softened
2 c. all-purpose flour
1 t. vanilla extract

1 c. powdered sugar
1 c. walnuts, finely chopped
Garnish: powdered sugar

In a large bowl, combine all ingredients; roll into 1-1/2 inch balls. Place on an ungreased baking sheet. Bake at 350 degrees for about 10 to 15 minutes. Roll in powdered sugar while still warm.

Create a pretty marbleized effect when baking a white cake.
Simply sprinkle batter in its pan with a few drops of
food coloring, then swirl the color around with a knife tip.

Tres Leches Cake

18-1/4 oz. pkg. yellow cake mix
14-oz. can sweetened condensed
   milk
5-oz. can evaporated milk
7.6-oz. can media crema or
   1 c. whole milk

8-oz. container frozen whipped
   topping, thawed
Optional: sliced fruit, such as
   strawberries, pineapple
   chunks, mandarin oranges
   and kiwi

Prepare cake mix according to package directions; bake in a 13"x9" baking pan. While cake is still warm, pierce surface all over with a toothpick or wooden skewer, about every 1/2 inch. Combine milks; pour over cake slowly and evenly. Allow cake to stand at room temperature for 30 minutes. Cover with plastic wrap or aluminum foil; refrigerate for at least 30 minutes, until well chilled. At serving time, frost cake with whipped topping; decorate with fruit, if using. Cut into squares. Keep refrigerated.

Make desserts extra-special. After placing servings
on dessert plates, drizzle with chocolate syrup,
caramel topping or raspberry syrup...so pretty!

Caramel Flan

3/4 c. sugar
12-oz. can evaporated milk
14-oz. can sweetened condensed
   milk

3 eggs
1 T. vanilla extract
Garnish: whipped cream,
   sliced fruit

Sprinkle sugar in a small, heavy saucepan. Heat and stir constantly over medium-low heat for 3 to 4 minutes, until melted and golden. Quickly pour into an ungreased 9" pie plate; swirl to coat bottom and sides. Use caution…the caramelized sugar is extremely hot. Combine milks, eggs and vanilla in a blender; cover and blend for one minute. Pour over sugar in pie plate. Set pie plate in a large roasting pan; fill roasting pan with one inch of warm water. Bake at 325 degrees for 45 to 50 minutes, until a knife inserted near center comes out clean. Cool on a wire rack for one hour; refrigerate for 4 to 6 hours, or until firm. To serve, quickly dip the pie plate into hot water; run a knife around the edge and invert onto a rimmed serving plate. Cut into wedges; garnish as desired.

Offer mini portions of a rich cake or pie in small glasses,
layered with whipped cream and a crunchy topping.
Everyone can take "just a taste" of something sweet
after a big dinner or sample several yummy treats.

Golden Tequila Lime Tart

Makes 24 servings

12 graham crackers, crushed
1/4 c. pine nuts
3 T. sugar, divided
1/2 c. butter, melted
14-oz. can sweetened condensed
    milk
1/2 c. lime juice
1/4 c. gold tequila or
    lemon-lime soda
4 egg yolks
2 egg whites
Garnish: whipped cream, lime
    slices

Process crackers finely in a food processor. Measure out 1-1/2 cups; set aside in a medium bowl. Finely grind nuts and 2 tablespoons sugar in food processor; stir nut mixture and butter into crumbs. Press mixture evenly onto bottom and up sides of an ungreased 9"x9" baking pan. In a large bowl, whisk together condensed milk, lime juice, tequila or soda and egg yolks until well blended. In another large bowl, beat egg whites and remaining sugar with an electric mixer on high speed until soft peaks form. Stir one-quarter of egg white mixture into milk mixture; gently fold in remaining egg white mixture until thoroughly combined. Spoon into crust. Bake at 325 degrees for 25 to 30 minutes, until edges of filling are puffed and light golden, and center is set. Cool completely on a wire rack; cover loosely and chill for 2 hours to overnight. Garnish as desired.

INDEX

INDEX

Our Story

Back in 1984, we were next-door neighbors raising our families in the little town of Delaware, Ohio. Two moms with small children, we were looking for a way to do what we loved and stay home with the kids too. We had always shared a love of home cooking and making memories with family & friends and so, after many a conversation over the backyard fence, **Gooseberry Patch** was born.

We put together our first catalog at our kitchen tables, enlisting the help of our loved ones wherever we could. From that very first mailing, we found an immediate connection with many of our customers and it wasn't long before we began receiving letters, photos and recipes from these new friends. In 1992, we put together our very first cookbook, compiled from hundreds of these recipes and, the rest, as they say, is history.

Hard to believe it's been over 25 years since those kitchen-table days! From that original little **Gooseberry Patch** family, we've grown to include an amazing group of creative folks who love cooking, decorating and creating as much as we do. Today, we're best known for our homestyle, family-friendly cookbooks, now recognized as national bestsellers.

One thing's for sure, we couldn't have done it without our friends all across the country. Each year, we're honored to turn thousands of your recipes into our collectible cookbooks. Our hope is that each book captures the stories and heart of all of you who have shared with us. Whether you've been with us since the beginning or are just discovering us, welcome to the **Gooseberry Patch** family!

Visit our website anytime
www.gooseberrypatch.com

JoAnn & Vickie

1·800·854·6673